EUROPEAN COUNTRIES TODAY
CZECH REPUBLIC

EUROPEAN COUNTRIES TODAY

TITLES IN THE SERIES

EUROPEAN COUNTRIES TODAY
CZECH REPUBLIC

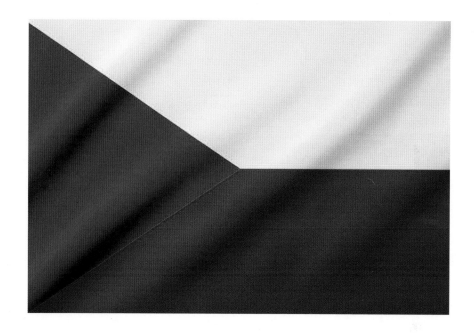

Dominic J. Ainsley

MASON CREST

Mason Crest
450 Parkway Drive, Suite D
Broomall, Pennsylvania PA 19008
(866) MCP-BOOK (toll free)

First printing
9 8 7 6 5 4 3 2 1

ISBN: 978-1-4222-3980-3
Series ISBN: 978-1-4222-3977-3
ebook ISBN: 978-1-4222-7795-9

Cataloging-in-Publication Data on file with the Library of Congress.

Printed in the United States of America

Cover images
Main: *Charles Bridge, Prague.*
Left: *Traditional foods of the Czech Republic.*
Center: *Křivoklát Castle, Central Bohemia.*
Right: *A couple in national dress.*

QR CODES AND LINKS TO THIRD-PARTY CONTENT

CONTENTS

KEY ICONS TO LOOK FOR:

 Words to Understand: These words with their easy-to-understand definitions will increase the reader's understanding of the text while building vocabulary skills.

 Sidebars: This boxed material within the main text allows readers to build knowledge, gain insights, explore possibilities, and broaden their perspectives by weaving together additional information to provide realistic and holistic perspectives.

 Educational Videos: Readers can view videos by scanning our QR codes, providing them with additional content to supplement the text. Examples include news coverage, moments in history, speeches, iconic sports moments, and much more!

 Text-Dependent Questions: These questions send the reader back to the text for more careful attention to the evidence presented there.

 Research Projects: Readers are pointed toward areas of further inquiry connected to each chapter. Suggestions are provided for projects that encourage deeper research and analysis.

THE CZECH REPUBLIC AT A GLANCE

MAP OF EUROPE

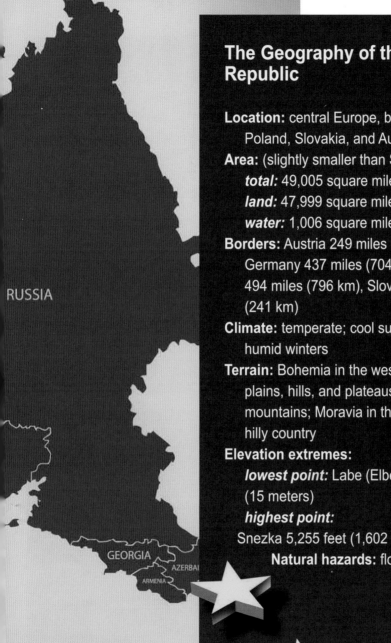

The Geography of the Czech Republic

Location: central Europe, between Germany, Poland, Slovakia, and Austria

Area: (slightly smaller than South Carolina)
total: 49,005 square miles (78,867 sq. km)
land: 47,999 square miles (77,247 sq. km)
water: 1,006 square miles (1,620 sq. km)

Borders: Austria 249 miles (402 km), Germany 437 miles (704 km), Poland 494 miles (796 km), Slovakia 149 miles (241 km)

Climate: temperate; cool summers; cold, cloudy, humid winters

Terrain: Bohemia in the west consists of rolling plains, hills, and plateaus surrounded by low mountains; Moravia in the east consists of very hilly country

Elevation extremes:
lowest point: Labe (Elbe) River 49 feet (15 meters)
highest point:
Snezka 5,255 feet (1,602 meters)
Natural hazards: flooding

Source: www.cia.gov 2017

Flag the of Czech Republic

The Czech Republic, formerly part of Czechoslovakia, consists of two areas: Bohemia to the west and Moravia to the east. In 1989 the Communist system was replaced by a multi party democracy. This was a difficult transition, and an upsurge of Slovak nationalism in 1992 resulted in the break-up of Czechoslovakia, although ultimately the split was amicable. The split took place on January 1, 1993, and the Czech Republic adopted the flag of the former Czechoslovakia. The red and white represent Bohemia, and the blue triangle Moravia and Slovakia.

ABOVE: *Small restaurants open for the evening in Prague Old Town. As in most major European cities, restaurants advertise their menus in English.*

The People of the Czech Republic

Population: 10,644,842 (July 2016 est.)
Ethnic Groups: Czech 64.3%, Moravian 5%, Slovak 1.4%
  other 1.8%, unspecified 27.5% (last census)
Age Structure:
  0–14 years: 15.09%
  15–24 years: 9.89%
  25–54 years: 43.79%
  55–64 years: 12.73%
  65 years and above: 18.5%
Population Growth Rate: 0.14% (2016 est.)
Birth Rate: 9.5 births/1,000 population (2016 est.)
Death Rate: 10.4 deaths/1,000 population (July 2016 est.)
Migration Rate: 2.3 migrant(s)/1,000 population (2016 est.)
Life Expectancy at Birth:
Total Population: 78.6 years
  Male: 75.7 years
  Female: 81.8 years (2016 est.)
Total Fertility Rate: 1.45 children born/woman (2016 est.)
Religions: Catholic 10.4%, Protestant 1.1%, unspecified 54%,
  none 34.5%
Languages: Czech 95.4%, Slovak 1.6%, other 3%
Literacy rate: 99%

Source: www.cia.gov 2017

Words to Understand

acid rain: Rain that has increased acidity caused by pollutants.

landlocked: A country enclosed by land.

spa: A resort with mineral springs.

BELOW: Loket Castle dates back to the thirteenth century. It was visited regularly by Charles IV, Holy Roman Emperor. It is situated in Sokolov, a town in the Karlovy Vary region.

Chapter One
THE CZECH REPUBLIC'S GEOGRAPHY & LANDSCAPE

Dobr den! Welcome to the Czech Republic. This new nation, nestled in the heart of Central Europe, has historically been a bridge between the nations of East and West. Now, as the formerly communist countries of Eastern Europe reach for the growth and prosperity of their neighbors to the west, the Czech Republic is poised to become a center for trade and education once again.

The Czech Republic is a small country, about the same size as the state of South Carolina. The country is **landlocked**, having no bordering seas, but it does border four other countries: Germany, Austria, Poland, and Slovakia.

ABOVE: *The Brno Reservoir was created by damming the Svratka River. The dam is located just outside the city of Brno, Moravia. The dam is used to generate hydroelectricity.*

Educational Video

This 10-minute video gives a brief insight into the Czech Republic's geography. Scan the QR code with your phone to watch!

Plains, Mountains, Valleys, and Forests

The Czech Republic features varied terrain, including mountains, plateaus, and low-lying plains.

Moravia, in the eastern part of the country, consists of rolling green hills, while rivers cross through the flatter central regions. These river valleys

ABOVE: *The Beskids Mountains form part of the Carpathian range.*

provided the soft fertile land that was so critical for the cultivation of crops when farming was the primary activity in the area. Bohemia, in the west, features low mountains. The highest Czech mountains are the Krkonoše, followed by the Hrubý Jeseník and the Šumava mountain range.

Approximately one-third of the Czech Republic is forested. These forests are mainly coniferous, or evergreen, and are home to many different species of plants and animals. Unfortunately, many areas of the country suffer from environmental damage. Although recent reforms have dramatically improved the country's environmental situation, air and water pollution remain a problem.

ABOVE: The Vltava River meandering through a densely forested region.

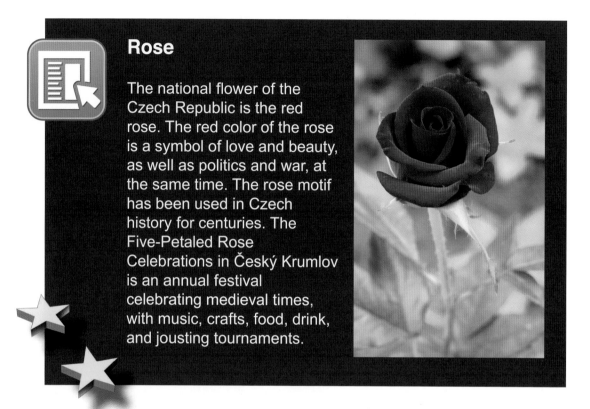

Rose

The national flower of the Czech Republic is the red rose. The red color of the rose is a symbol of love and beauty, as well as politics and war, at the same time. The rose motif has been used in Czech history for centuries. The Five-Petaled Rose Celebrations in Český Krumlov is an annual festival celebrating medieval times, with music, crafts, food, drink, and jousting tournaments.

Acid rain, caused by harmful industrial emissions, is damaging Czech forests. The most heavily damaged region, in northern Bohemia, is known as the "Black Triangle" due to the environmental damage inflicted by factories there.

Rivers and Lakes

The Czech Republic features four major navigable rivers, the Elbe, Vltava, Morava, and the Ohře. Historically, these rivers have provided a crucial means of transport for people and goods, and most of the country's cities have grown up around the rivers as transportation centers.

The Czech Republic also boasts more than four hundred lakes and a large number of natural mineral springs. These mineral springs, long believed to have healing properties, have spawned a thriving tourism industry centered on alternative medicine. People from all over visit these Czech **spa** towns to bathe in the mineral springs.

ABOVE: *The Krkonoše National Park spans the Liberec and Hradec Králové regions of the Czech Republic.*

ABOVE: *The peregrine falcon is endangered, but still present in the Czech Republic.*

Red Fox

A widespread and commonly found species in the Czech Republic, the red fox is found in both urban and rural areas. In the countryside, foxes are found around farmland, woodland, and hillsides. When not hunting, they usually lie up in an underground burrow either one taken over from another animal or one they have dug themselves.
Courtship occurs in the dark months of winter, when the animals' eerie, barking calls are frequently to be heard. The young are born blind in the underground earths, and the vixen (female) guards them while the dog (male) hunts for food for the family. The cubs learn to hunt by playing and practicing pouncing.

A Temperate Climate

The Czech Republic has a cool, wet, temperate climate. Summers are cloudy, and winters are cold, humid, and generally overcast.

Trees, Plants, and Wildlife

As mentioned earlier, one-third of the Czech Republic is wooded. While most of the woodlands are comprised of coniferous trees like spruce and fir, some varieties of deciduous trees can be found as well. (Deciduous trees are trees that shed their leaves when cool weather approaches.) Some examples of deciduous trees native to the region include beech, birch, and oak. Wild flowers and berries are abundant across the countryside.

Czech wildlife includes deer, wild boars, hares, wolves, and foxes. The lynx, an endangered species, is also native to the region. The peregrine falcon, another endangered animal, also inhabits Czech lands. Other birds found in the area include various types of eagles, kites, owls, and storks.

The Czech Republic is truly a land of great natural wealth. The country has provided a cradle for many important species important throughout Europe.

ABOVE: *Telč is an ancient town in the region of Moravia.*

ABOVE: *Pravčická Brána is a large natural stone arch in the Bohemian Switzerland National Park in the far north of the Bohemia region.*

The Czech Republic's Regions
Bohemia
The region of Bohemia encompasses the west of the Czech Republic. Prague, the capital, is situated in the center of the region. Prague is famous for its Gothic Charles Bridge, the Old Town Square, and Prague Castle. The Vltava River flows south from the city through the town of České Budějovice, home of the Budvar brewery, and the medieval town of Český Krumlov, which is known for its picturesque pub-lined streets and castle.

Moravia
Moravia is situated in the eastern side of the Czech Republic. The land takes its name from the Morava River that is the region's major waterway. It rises in the far north of the region and flows southward to the border with Slovakia. Moravia's largest city and historical capital is Brno. Though officially abolished by an administrative reform in 1949, Moravia is still commonly acknowledged as a specific region in the Czech Republic. Moravian people are proud of their

Moravian identity and therefore there is often rivalry between them and the Czechs from Bohemia.

Czech Silesia

Czech Silesia lies to the northeast of the Czech Republic and is the smallest of the historical regions. It borders Moravia to the south, and the city of Ostrava is roughly in its geographic center. After Ostrava, the most important cities are Opava and Český Těšín. Today, much of the modern region of Moravian-Silesia (save for its southern edges) corresponds to the historic region, along with a small part of the Olomouc region around the city of Jeseník in the far west.

Situated in the Sudeten mountains, the region is cornered by the Carpathians in the east. Its major rivers are the Oder, Opava, and Olše, which form part of the natural border with Poland.The country we recognize today as the Czech Republic is a new nation, formed on January 1, 1993, when the former Czechoslovakia separated, creating two new countries—the Czech Republic and Slovakia. Although the Czech Republic is an infant nation, its land and people have a rich and ancient history.

ABOVE: *Skyline of Brno, a large city in Moravia.*

ABOVE: *Masaryk Square, Ostrava, which is the largest town in Czech Silesia.*

Text-Dependent Questions

1. How large is the Czech Republic?

2. What is the "Black Triangle" in the north of Bohemia?

3. What is the most important river in Moravia?

Research Project

The Czech Republic has many sites entered on the UNESCO World Heritage list. Find out about five of the most important ones and write a description of each.

Words to Understand

Celts: A group of people who lived in ancient Britain and parts of western Europe.

hereditary: Relating to the possession of a title or lands through inheritance or by reason of birth.

Holy Roman Empire: An empire consisting of a loose confederation of German and Italian territories existing from 800 CE to 1806.

The Vltava River flows through central Bohemia. The name Vltava is said to have derived from the Celtic words "Vit" and "Va," meaning "wild" and "water."

Chapter Two
THE GOVERNMENT & HISTORY OF THE CZECH REPUBLIC

The country we recognize today as the Czech Republic is a new nation, formed on January 1, 1993, when the former Czechoslovakia separated, creating two new countries: the Czech Republic and Slovakia. Although the Czech Republic is an infant nation, its land and people have a rich and ancient history.

Czech Lands in Ancient Times

Human settlement of modern-day Czech lands was first recorded around 400 BCE, with the arrival of **Celts** from western Europe. Ancient Romans called the region "Boiohaemum" after the Boii Celts who occupied the area. This name stuck, as people still refer to the western region of the Czech Republic as "Bohemia." Although the Boii were partially chased out of the region by invading Germanic tribes, they left a lasting influence on the culture and language of the area. One example is the Czech name for the Moldau River, which runs through the capital city of Prague. Czechs call the river "Vltava," which is said to have come from the Celtic words "Vit" and "Va," meaning "wild" and "water."

By 600 CE, Slavic people fully inhabited the area, having migrated in waves from the

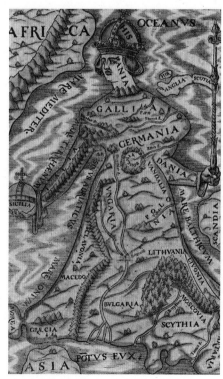

ABOVE: *A famous cartographic oddity showing Europe portrayed as a queen with Bohemia as her heart. Printed in 1570 by Sebastian Münster.*

Educational Video

A fun and interesting video about the Czech Republic and the Czech People.

east. A century later, a Frankish merchant named Samo united the people of the territory in the first recorded state. This early state collapsed shortly after Samo's death, and the area remained unstable until the ninth century. Czechs were next briefly united with their Slovak neighbors as part of the Great Moravian Empire, established by the Slavic leader Mojmir. Around this time, the Přemyslid family established the Bohemian Kingdom, joining the various Czech tribes in Bohemia, Moravia, and Silesia under stable feudal rule.

The Bohemian Kingdom

As the Great Moravian Empire disintegrated by the tenth century, a new political entity, the Bohemian Kingdom, emerged. It would play an important role in the development of the Czech nation. The Bohemian Kingdom was a major medieval political, economic, and cultural entity and is now viewed by many Czechs as one of the brightest periods of their country's history.

Over the centuries, the Přemyslid family accumulated land, wealth, and power, eventually extending the Bohemian

ABOVE: *Mojmir of Moravia.*

24

Kingdom from areas in modern-day Austria all the way to the Adriatic Sea. The young Přemyslid state maintained its sovereignty, even though it officially recognized the feudal authority of the **Holy Roman Empire**.

The Holy Roman Empire was a group of European territories that stood united by their common faith in the Roman Catholic Church, under the rule of one supreme emperor. Individual territories had their own rulers, each of whom acknowledged the authority of the emperor through the payment of tribute and military alliances.

As the Bohemian Empire expanded, the Czech people were exposed to strong German and Roman Catholic influences through their allegiance to the empire. As the population swelled and trade flourished, Czech lands soon came to be

ABOVE: *King Přemysl Otakar I of Bohemia on a relief, from the St. George Convent in Prague Castle.*

counted among the richest of the European feudal states. And as the wealth of the region expanded, the Přemyslid family and the regional nobility sought to increase their power and independence.

In 1212, King Přemysl Otakar I received the Golden Bull of Sicily (a formal decree) from the Holy Roman Emperor Frederick II, confirming the royal title of "king" for Otakar and his descendants. Previously, the emperor had had the power to appoint or remove any new ruler. The king's successor, Přemysl Otakar II, married a German princess, Margaret of Babenberg, and became duke of Austria and acquired large amounts of land in central Europe. From 1273, however, the Habsburg emperor Rudolf began to reassert his authority. All Přemysl Otakar II's German possessions were lost in 1276, and in 1278, he died in battle against the emperor.

By 1306, the Přemyslid line had died out, and John of Luxembourg claimed the Czech throne. The reign of his son, King Charles IV who was raised in the French court, is widely acknowledged as the Golden Age of Czech history.

Charles IV was crowned Holy Roman Emperor in 1355. The Bohemian Kingdom ceased to be a fief of the emperor, and Prague became the new imperial city. During his reign as King of Bohemia, Charles implemented building projects over the entire region, including a major renovation of Hradčany, the royal castle. Charles University was founded in 1348 and helped cement Prague's status as a leading international center of culture and learning.

In the centuries that followed, the Czech people endured great political and religious upheaval. This period, during which the Protestant Reformation swept across

ABOVE: *The death of John of Luxembourg in 1346 at the Battle of Crécy, France.*

Europe, saw a series of anti-Catholic and anti-German revolts as people began to question the authority of the Roman Catholic Church. A sizable number of Germans had migrated to the region during the growth of the Bohemian Empire, and now cultural and ethnic differences between Germans and Czechs added fuel to religious conflicts.

Czechs who were opposed to the practices of the Catholic Church were known as Hussites, after the early Czech reformer Jan Hus, who was burned at the stake by Catholics for his views. The Hussite movement gained momentum, and its followers eventually defeated five separate waves of Catholic crusaders. But then they began warring with one another over economic and social divisions.

The political situation was very volatile, and power would change hands many times before stable, effective rule was eventually reestablished. This began when Bohemia first came under the rule of the Habsburg family of Austria. Although the first Habsburg ruler, King Ferdinand, took control of the Bohemian throne in 1526, rebellion and religious wars continued to plague the territory until Habsburg forces decisively defeated Czech troops at the Battle of White Mountain on November 8, 1620.

Habsburg Rule

The Habsburg victory over Czech forces in 1620 was followed by strict new measures that ensured the absolute rule of the Habsburg dynasty and the supremacy of the Roman Catholic Church in the region. All Czech lands were declared **hereditary** property of the Habsburg family, and all law was issued by royal decree. Many native Czech nobles were executed; most of the rest fled, their lands confiscated by the crown.

ABOVE: *Charles IV, Holy Roman Emperor.*

Many German Catholics immigrated to the area and became the new Bohemian nobility. The entire educational system, including Charles University, was placed under Catholic control. German became the dominant language of the region. The Habsburg policy of centralization ultimately cost the Czechs most of their native aristocracy, their reformed religion, and even the common use of their native language.

By the eighteenth century, all that remained of the Bohemian Kingdom had been merged into the Austrian provinces of the Habsburg realm. During this period, known as the Age of Enlightenment, Europe saw remarkable cultural changes characterized by a loss of faith in traditional religious sources of authority and a turn toward human rights, science, and rational thought. Habsburg rulers Maria-Theresa and her son Joseph II instituted reforms based

ABOVE: *Maria Theresa by Martin van Meytens.*

on Enlightenment principles to promote social and economic progress.

The consequences of Enlightenment reforms were widespread. The power and authority of the Catholic Church were reduced, and some freedom of worship was established. Catholic control of education came to a halt, and the focus of study shifted from theology to the sciences. Feudalism was modified, so serfs could marry and change residences without obtaining the lord's consent.

Eventually, the nobility shifted their focus from agriculture to industry, investing their profits in coal mining and manufacturing. This freed Czech peasants from the land, and enabled the migration of workers from the countryside to urban centers. The sons of these peasants were educated, and for the first time some attended the university. The increased educational and economic opportunities presented by the Enlightenment-era reforms set the stage for a resurgence of Czech culture.

Czech Nationalism

The dawn of the nineteenth century marked a period of national awakening across Central Europe. The aggression of the French general Napoleon Bonaparte created a wave of nationalism among Germans. The concept of a nation as a group people linked by a common language and culture had great appeal to the Czech people, who had lived for centuries under foreign rule. Inspired by the renewed interest in German national identity that was taking place among their neighbors, the Czech intellectual elite soon launched a national revival of their own.

ABOVE: *Joseph II (right) with his brother Peter Leopold, then Grand Duke of Tuscany, later Emperor Leopold II, by Pompeo Batoni.*

ABOVE: Emperor Francis Joseph.

Initial national movements were limited to discussions of language, literature, and culture. The Czech language, by this time, existed only as a peasant dialect. Scholars began their first attempts at recording the Czech language and introduced the study of Czech language in state schools. The Museum of the Bohemian Kingdom (now known as the National Museum) was established in 1818 and served as a center for Czech scholarly activity.

Nationalist feeling soon expanded beyond scholarly pursuits, and Czech nationalists began to form political alliances as well. Czechs reached out to other Slavic peoples, such as the Slovaks, Poles, Slovenians, Croats, Ukrainians, and Serbs, with whom they shared a common ethnic identity.

By 1848, the Habsburgs were seeing a series of nationalist demonstrations and revolts across their lands. In 1859 they were driven out of Italy, and by 1866 they were defeated by Germany and expelled from the German Confederation. To strengthen his political power base, Habsburg Emperor Francis Joseph reached out to the Hungarian nobility and in 1867 created the Austro-Hungarian Empire. Austria and Hungary were now united by a common ruler, but were otherwise independent states, each with a separate parliament and judicial system. Political power rested with ethnic Germans in Austria and Hungarians in Hungary. Czechs were eventually allowed greater political involvement in the Austrian half of the empire, and this process peaked when all men were given the right to vote in 1907. In neighboring Hungary, however, the Slovak population were continually denied the right to participate in their government.

ABOVE: *Archduke Franz Ferdinand, his wife Sophie, and their children.*

World War I and the Czechoslovak Republic

The inability of the Austro-Hungarian Empire to ease tensions between the different nationalities under its rule eventually led to the its fall. World War I began on June 28, 1914, when Gavrilo Princip, a Serbian nationalist, assassinated Austrian Archduke Franz Ferdinand and his wife Sophie. Russia allied with Serbia. Germany sided with Austria and soon declared war on Russia. After France declared its support for Russia, Germany attacked France. German troops then invaded Belgium, a neutral country, as it stood between German forces and Paris. Great Britain declared war on Germany.

Czechs and Slovaks had little interest in fighting for their oppressors, the Germans and Hungarians, against Russians and Serbians, who were fellow Slavs. Czech and Slovak troops deserted the German army on the Russian front and formed the Czechoslovak Legion. Germany and Austria proposed peace negotiations in early October 1918, and on October 28, 1918, the Czechoslovak National Council in Prague proclaimed the independence of Czechoslovakia.

When the Paris Peace Conference opened in January 1919, the provisional Czechoslovak government was represented. The victorious allies formally recognized the Czechoslovak Republic and established its borders. The new republic would cover the lands of the historic Bohemian Kingdom, Slovakia, and an area called Ruthenia, thus gaining a common border with Romania. The new nation had a population of over 13.5 million. It also inherited between 70 and 80 percent of all industries formerly held by the Austro-Hungarian Empire, making the infant democracy one of the world's ten most industrialized states.

ABOVE: *Gavrilo Princip, who assassinated Archduke Franz Ferdinand and his wife Sophie in Serbia, sparking World War I.*

One problem that plagued the new republic was the dissatisfaction of the German minority. Once in control of much of the wealth, land, and political power of the region, the Germans resented their smaller role in the new government. Most of these Germans occupied a region known as the Sudetenland on Czechoslovakia's western border. The grievances of this minority German population would come to serve as a pretext for the eventual Nazi takeover of Czechoslovakia.

ABOVE: Hitler forced Czechoslovakia to surrender the Sudetenland.

World War II and the Rise of Communism

By 1933, Adolph Hitler had come to power in nearby Germany, and by 1938, he had occupied neighboring Austria as well. His stated objective was to unify all ethnic Germans. He soon demanded the surrender of Czechoslovakia's Sudetenland, taking up the cause of the Sudeten Germans. On September 29, 1938, France, Germany, Italy, and Great Britain signed the Munich Agreement, demanding that Czechoslovakia surrender the Sudetenland to Germany in exchange for a promise of peace. However, in March 1939, Hitler reneged on his agreement and invaded the remainder of Czechoslovakia.

Czechoslovakia was reestablished in 1945, after the defeat of Nazi Germany. It retained all of its 1938 boundaries except for the province of Ruthenia, which was ceded to the Soviet Union. Although democracy was briefly reintroduced, the new government was unstable.

The Soviet Army was a strong presence in Eastern Europe in the years following World War II. Taking advantage of their great influence, Communists maneuvered to gain political power by obtaining key government positions. By 1948, the Soviets had taken over completely, and Czechoslovakia was converted into a satellite nation of the Soviet Union. Under communism, all private ownership of land and industry was outlawed. Every aspect of Czech life was now under the direct control of the government.

Resistance and Reform

By the late 1960s, key changes had occurred in Czechoslovakian communist leadership. In March 1968, the Communist Party announced a radical policy of liberalization called "Socialism with a Human Face." The rapid spread of democratization that followed became known as the "Prague Spring." The Soviet Union acted quickly to put down the movement, sending 600,000 troops from neighboring communist countries to occupy Czechoslovakia and force an end to the movement. A harsh communist government was installed whose repressive policies were intended to prevent any further attempts at reform. This government would rule unchallenged for two decades.

Communism in Czechoslovakia

Czechoslovakia was occupied by Germany during World War II, but the Communists emerged as the strongest party in 1946, and by 1948 their grip on the country had tightened. During the era of Communist Party rule, thousands of Czechoslovaks faced political persecution for various offenses, such as trying to emigrate across the Iron Curtain. However, there was brief period of liberalization in 1968 (the Prague Spring), during which a program of political, economic, and cultural reforms was initiated, but ended in failure. However the "Velvet Revolution" of 1989 ensured a relatively painless transition towards a non-Communist government.

ABOVE: *A bust of Joseph Stalin, leader of the Communist Party of the USSR, is located at the Museum of Communism in Prague.*

Sweeping political changes were taking place across Eastern Europe by the late 1980s. Inspired by events in East Germany, Poland, and the Soviet Union itself, demonstrators swarmed the streets of Prague in November 1989, demanding political and economic reforms. This is known in Czech history as the "Velvet Revolution" due to the smooth transition of power and the fact that no blood was shed in earning Czech independence from Soviet control.

In June 1990, free elections were held for the first time in forty-two years. By 1992, a democratic government had been established, and voters passed a referendum ending the political union of Czechs and Slovaks. On January 1, 1993, Czechoslovakia ceased to exist and the Czech Republic was born.

ABOVE: *The Czech Republic embraces capitalism. Palladium is a shopping mall located in the center of Prague.*

ABOVE: *Wallenstein Palace is a baroque palace in Lesser Town (Malá Strana), Prague. It is currently the home of the Czech Senate.*

ABOVE: *Modern Prague–The Dancing House, nicknamed Ginger and Fred, was built by architects Vlado Milunić (Czech) and Frank Gehry (American) in 1992. It was finished in 1996.*

The Czech Republic Today

The Czech Republic has emerged from Soviet control to become a vibrant and growing member of the international community. It now has one of Europe's most open markets and leads all the former Soviet satellite states in economic growth. Membership in the European Union (EU) has further increased trade and established the Czech Republic in the international arena.

Czechs now actively participate in government, with thirteen different political parties having participated in the most recent election. Every citizen over the age of eighteen has the right to vote. The national constitution guarantees civil rights to all citizens. While problems still exist, the Czech Republic as a whole has emerged from centuries of conflict and foreign rule to become a free country with a clear sense of national identity.

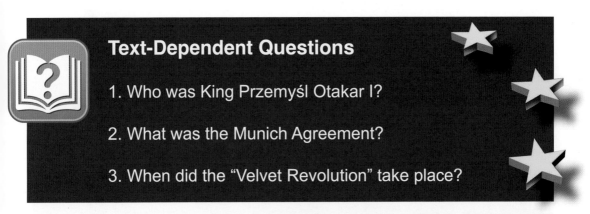

Text-Dependent Questions

1. Who was King Przemyśl Otakar I?

2. What was the Munich Agreement?

3. When did the "Velvet Revolution" take place?

Research Project

Research and then write an essay about Czechoslovakia's role during World War II.

The Formation of the European Union (EU)

The EU is a confederation of European nations that continues to grow. As of 2017, there are twenty-eight official members. Several other candidates are also waiting for approval. All countries that enter the EU agree to follow common laws about foreign security policies. They also agree to cooperate on legal matters that go on within the EU. The European Council meets to discuss all international matters and make decisions about them. Each country's own concerns and interests are important, though. And apart from legal and financial issues, the EU tries to uphold values such as peace, human dignity, freedom, and equality.

All member countries remain autonomous. This means that they generally keep their own laws and regulations. The idea for a union among European nations was first mentioned after World War II. The war had devastated much of Europe, both physically and financially. In 1950, the French foreign minister suggested that France and West Germany combine their coal and steel industries under one authority. Both countries would have control over the

ABOVE: The entrance to the European Union Parliament Building in Brussels.

Member Countries

Austria	Greece	Romania
Belgium	Hungary	Slovakia
Bulgaria	Ireland	Slovenia
Croatia	Italy	Spain
Cyprus	Latvia	Sweden
Czech Republic	Lithuania	United Kingdom
Denmark	Luxembourg	*(Brexit: For the time*
Estonia	Malta	*being, the United*
Finland	Netherlands	*Kingdom remains a full*
France	Poland	*member of the EU.)*
Germany	Portugal	

industries. This would help them become more financially stable. It would also make war between the countries much more difficult. The idea was interesting to other European countries as well. In 1951, France, West Germany, Belgium, Luxembourg, the Netherlands, and Italy signed the Treaty of Paris, creating the European Coal and Steel Community. These six countries would become the core of the EU.

In 1957, these same countries signed the Treaties of Rome, creating the European Economic Community. In 1965, the Merger Treaty formed the European Community. Finally, in 1992, the Maastricht Treaty was signed. This treaty defined the European Union. It gave a framework for expanding the EU's political role, particularly in the area of foreign and security policy. It would also replace national currencies with the euro. The next year, the treaty went into effect. At that time, the member countries included the original six plus another six who had joined during the 1970s and '80s.

In the following years, the EU would take more steps to form a single market for its members. This would make joining the union even more advantageous. In addition to enlargement, the EU is steadily becoming more integrated through its own policies for closer cooperation between member states.

Words to Understand

infrastructure: The system of public works of a country including: buildings, roads, equipment, personnel, etc.

investment: The outlay of money for income or profit.

privatize: To change from public to private control or ownership.

BELOW: Vineyards in Pálava, Moravia. Wine in the Czech Republic is produced mainly in southern Moravia, although a few vineyards are located in Bohemia. Production centers on local grape varieties, but there has been an increase in the production of established international strains such as Cabernet Sauvignon.

Chapter Three
THE CZECH REPUBLIC'S ECONOMY

Of all the developing democracies in Eastern Europe, the Czech Republic is one of the fastest-growing economies in the region. Since its independence from Soviet control, the Czech Republic has struggled to overcome the loss of favorable trade with former communist countries to the east, some of which still owe the former Czechoslovakia substantial debts. However, the Czech Republic is now steadily emerging from that difficult economic past to be the successful and modern country it is today.

ABOVE: *The Devil's Stairs quarry (Velkolom Čertovy schody) is a vast limestone quarry near Prague.*

A Developing Economy

Primary industries in the Czech Republic remain much the same today as under communism. Heavy and general machine building makes up the largest sector of industry, followed closely by iron and steel production, metalworking, chemical production, transportation equipment, textiles, glass, brewing, electronics, china, ceramics, and pharmaceuticals. The country has a strong industrial heritage dating back to the days when Bohemia was the industrial base of the Austro-Hungarian Empire. Unfortunately, although the country has an educated and capable workforce and solid **infrastructure**, many of its factories were neglected during the communist years. Fortunately though, since 2004, EU membership and more foreign **investment** has strengthened its economy to allow new industries to develop, and in new regions too.

ABOVE: *Glass manufacturing in Svojkov. The Czech Republic has a long history of glass production.*

Bohemian Glass

Glassmaking has been present in the Czech Republic since the thirteenth century, and it originated in the regions of Bohemia and Silesia. Those regions have vast natural sand deposits and wood, both of which were traditionally used in glassmaking. Bohemian glass is internationally recognized for its craftsmanship, quality, beauty, and design. The best glassware is cut, engraved, blown, and decorated by hand. Items such as chandeliers, figurines, ornaments, and drinking glasses are exported throughout the world. Given the long history of glass and crystal production in the country, it is hardly surprising that Bohemian glass now ranks among the world's best.

ABOVE: *Decorative glass known as "Bohemian glass" is one of the Czech Republic's lucrative exports. This glassware is on sale in a gift shop in Prague.*

Agriculture

The Czech Republic is now primarily an urban industrial society rather than an agrarian one. Farming today is mainly used to meet local demand, and currently makes up only 3 percent of the total gross domestic product (GDP). The leading crops produced are sugar beet, potatoes, wheat, and hops for the thriving domestic brewing industry.

Energy Sources

Heavily dependent on polluting brown coal as a source of energy, the Czech government is investing in developing cleaner, more efficient sources of energy. Currently, about 25 percent of the country's energy needs are met through nuclear power, although that figure is expected to rise to as high as 40 percent in the near future. Natural

ABOVE: *Hops are an important ingredient in the production of Czech beer.*

Educational Video

This video explains why the automotive sector is the backbone of Czech industry.

ABOVE: *The cooling towers of the nuclear power plant at Temelín.*

gas is also a critical source of energy, and the country currently imports most of its gas via pipelines from Norway and Russia. Oil is imported from foreign lands as well.

Transportation

Transportation in the Czech Republic occurs mainly via highway or rail. The country's important navigable rivers the Elbe, the Vltava, the Morava, and the Oder also provide water transportation. Air travel is available at 91 airports nationwide, including 5 large international airports.

ABOVE: The Czech Republic relies on rail networks for moving freight. This is a diesel electric locomotive.

The Economy of the Czech Republic

Gross Domestic Product (GDP): $353.9 billion (2016 est.)
GDP Per Capita: $33,200 (2016 est.)
Industries: motor vehicles, metallurgy, machinery and
equipment, glass, armaments
Agriculture: wheat, potatoes, sugar beet, fruit, pigs,
poultry
Export Commodities: machinery and transport equipment,
raw materials, fuel, chemicals
Export Partners: Germany 32.4%, Slovakia 9%, Poland
5.8%, UK 5.3%, France 5.1%, Italy 4.3, Austria 4.1%
Import Commodities: machinery and transport equipment,
raw materials and fuels, chemicals
Import Partners: Germany 26.4%, China 12.4%, Poland
8.3%, Slovakia 5.1%, Italy 4.2%
Currency: koruna

Source: www.cia.gov 2017

A Shift in Trade and Investment

Profound changes have been made in all aspects of the Czech economy.
A conscious effort has been made to look west rather than toward the old
economic partners in the east for investment and trade. Significant
improvements have been made in the areas of telecommunications and
banking to facilitate foreign investment in Czech enterprise, and business laws
and practices have been overhauled to meet Western standards.

The new republic has successfully managed to **privatize** most of the
country's industries through a unique voucher program. With the voucher
system, each citizen has an opportunity to buy, at an affordable price, a book of

ABOVE: *Renovated prefabricated apartments in Pilsen which date back to the communist era.*

industrial vouchers. Each voucher represents a potential share in a previously state-owned company. Holders then invest their vouchers in a specific company, providing needed money, which in turn helps to increase the stability of the company and the economic value of each individual share. Now completed, the program has made the Czech people some of the highest per capita shareholders in the world. By August 2015, Czech GDP growth was 4.4%, making the Czech economy the fastest growing in Europe.

Domestic demand is also playing an important role in fueling the expansion of the Czech economy. Credit cards and mortgages have become more easily available, and interest rates are beginning to fall, creating an increased demand for housing, consumer goods, and services. In fact, according to a recent estimate, service industries make up more than 50 percent of the GDP.

Although some problems persist, the Czech Republic has become one of the most prosperous states in Eastern Europe. Recent growth has been accelerated through an increase in exports to the EU, and foreign investment in Czech enterprise has nearly doubled in recent years. Continued governmental restructuring of banking, communications, and utilities will be needed to ensure continued economic development. Since joining the EU, economic conditions have been brought into harmony with the rest of the country's EU partners, which is a critical step in promoting continued growth and prosperity. As of 2016, the Czech Republic has the second lowest poverty rate of OECD members behind only Denmark.

Text-Dependent Questions

1. What are the Czech Republic's main industries?

2. How many international airports are there in the Czech Republic?

3. Why is the EU so important to the Czech Republic?

Research Project

The Czech Republic hosts one of the highest concentrations of automotive-related manufacturing and design activity in the world. Explain in detail why this industry is so successful.

Words to Understand

academic: Formal study especially at an institution of higher learning.

atheism: A lack of belief in the existence of a god or any gods.

literate: Able to read and write.

BELOW: Český Krumlov is a Bohemian town. The well-preserved castle dates back to the fourteenth century. It is a national monument and is included on the list of UNESCO World Cultural Heritage.

Chapter Four
CITIZENS OF
THE CZECH REPUBLIC: PEOPLE,
CUSTOMS & CULTURE

Most of the more than ten million people living in the Czech Republic today identify themselves as ethnic Czechs. Moravians, Slovaks, Poles, Germans, Silesians, Hungarians, and Roma (often called Gypsies) make up the non-Czech minority. The country's official language is Czech, and the Czech people are highly literate. Daily life in the Czech Republic looks much like life across Western Europe, and the people are very fond of literature, music, and the arts.

Religion
People living in the Czech Republic today enjoy full freedom of religion. Historically, Christianity was the dominant faith in the region, although this changed when the area came under communist control. Under communism, all public practice of religion was outlawed. It is no wonder that today, after forty years of enforced atheism, almost 40 percent of Czechs still identify themselves as atheists. Nearly as many identify themselves as Roman Catholics, while the remainder of the population is primarily undecided or affiliated with a Christian Protestant denomination. A small community of Czech Jews also exists. Estimated at about 10,000 people, most of this Jewish community is centered in the famous Josefov district of Prague. It is estimated that as many as 360,000 Jews were settled in Czech lands prior to the Nazi invasion of World War II.

Education and Sports
Czechs are a highly literate people. More than 99 percent of adults can read and write, and most of those adults are able to speak more than one language. National pride runs deep, fueling a trend toward building a competitive edge in both the arenas of education and athletics.

ABOVE: *Jana Opletala Gymnázium in Litovel, which is a town in the Olomouc region.*

This drive to be more competitive with the rest of the Western world has spurred a comprehensive reform of the Czech educational system. Since 2003, changes have been made to bring all schools nationwide into compliance with a new set of **academic** standards and streamline educational funding and administration. All children between three and six years of age can attend free nursery school, called *mateřská škola*. The majority of Czech children do attend, although attendance is not compulsory until age six. Then all children attend primary school, called *základni škola*, until age eleven. At age eleven, students have the option of studying at one of three different types of schools. *gymnázium*, which is similar to college-bound high schools in the United States, is the school of choice for the top 10 percent of Czech students. By law, class size in the *gymnázium* is limited to thirty students or less, and the curriculum is

Educational Video

A video about studying in the Czech Republic.

ABOVE: *Czech school children playing soccer in a Prague Football Association tournament.*

determined by strict national standards. Other students may opt to attend a technical school, *střední odborná škola*, or a vocational school, *střední odborné uèiliští*.

National pride is evident in the way Czechs approach competitive sports as well. In 1998, the Czech Republic national ice hockey team won Olympic gold, earning them the nickname the "Golden Boys of Nagano." The current national team is ranked sixth in the world. Soccer, known as *fotbal*, is hugely popular with Czech fans. Pavel Nedvěd, a native Czech, now retired, was voted European Player of the Year in 2003. Tennis is also a favorite sport.

ABOVE: *Martina Navratilova, one of the greatest female tennis players of all time, was born in Prague, but later moved to the United States where she turned professional.*

ABOVE: *The Czech Republic ice hockey team playing Sweden in the World Legends Hockey League.*

Food and Drink

Most traditional Czech meals consist of meat served with potatoes, dumplings, or cabbage. Beef and pork are favorites, and they are most commonly served fried of roasted. Typical eating habits feature a light breakfast and evening meal, with the main meal being served for lunch in the middle of the day. Some favorite national dishes include:

Svíčková: a beef pot roast served in a creamy vegetable sauce with dumplings
Bramboráky: deep-fried potato pancakes
Vepřo knedlo zelo: pork with dumplings and cabbage

As far as beverages are concerned, a popular Czech proverb says it all: *Kde se pivo vaří tam se dobře daří* (Where beer is brewed, they have it good). Czechs are the largest per-capita drinkers of beer in the world, consuming on average the equivalent of one bottle of beer for every man, woman, and child in the Czech Republic every day. Beer drinking was one of the few leisure activities to remain legal under communism, and the nation remains very proud of its beer industry.

Archaeological evidence suggests that hops, the critical ingredient for producing beer, were being cultivated in Czech lands as early as 859 CE and were being exported by 903 CE. By the eighteenth century, the world's first beer brewing textbook was written by Czech brewer, František Ondřej Poupě, a pioneer in many aspects of beer production. Breweries around the world later adopted his methods, including the introduction of thermometers and other scientific gauges to the brewing process.

Beer drinking is a central element of Czech culture. Pubs and country

ABOVE: *Vepřo knedlo zelo is a classic Bohemian dish.*

Moravian Christmas Cookies

This sweet and slightly spicy cookie is a favorite at holiday time. Czech children enjoy cutting these delicious treats into festive shapes.

Yields several dozen cookies, depending on the size of cookie cutters used.

Ingredients
8 oz. dark molasses
½ cup brown sugar
½ cup margarine
1½ teaspoons cinnamon
1½ teaspoons cloves
1 teaspoon ginger
1 teaspoon allspice
½ teaspoon nutmeg
1 tablespoon baking soda
4 cups flour

Directions
Mix flour, sugar, butter, and spices together. Heat molasses until lukewarm and add baking soda. Add molasses mixture to rest of ingredients and mix well. If necessary, add a little water to the dough to obtain a soft consistency. Roll the dough on a floured surface, making it as thin as possible. Cut into desired shapes, and transfer to a nonstick cookie sheet. Bake at 350 degrees for 6 to 8 minutes.

Bublanina (Czech Plum Squares)
12 servings

Ingredients
2 eggs, separated
½ cup butter, softened
½ cup sugar
1 cup flour, sifted with salt
½ teaspoon salt
½ teaspoon lemon rind
½ teaspoon cream of tartar
1 pound of plums, cut in quarters

Directions
Combine the butter, sugar, and egg yolks in a bowl and beat until very light and fluffy. In another bowl, add cream of tartar to egg whites and beat until it forms stiff peaks (be sure to clean the beaters thoroughly before beating the egg whites). Fold in flour alternately with egg whites into butter, sugar, egg yolk mixture. Spoon batter onto a baking sheet and cover with fruit. Bake at 400 degrees for 35 minutes.

inns provide a place for friends to meet and a forum in which to discuss everything from hockey to politics. Most pubs feature only local brews; foreign imports make up less than 1 percent of total Czech consumption. Czechs are fiercely loyal to their own national brews, some of which have been produced locally for centuries. One popular Czech brand, Budvar (pronounced like the similarly named American brew, Budweiser) has been a favorite of Czech royalty and common people alike since the sixteenth century. The word *Pilsener*, a common term for a broad range of classic, paler beers, actually comes from the Czech town of Pilsen. Today, a house in downtown Pilsen is home to the world's oldest beer museum.

ABOVE: *The town of Pilsen is where the famous Pilsener-style pale beer originates.*

ABOVE: *The Plzeňský Prazdroj Brewery was founded in 1842 and still produces beer today.*

The Czech Republic's Castles

The Czech Republic is known for its beautiful and impressive castles and châteaux, many of which have been well preserved throughout the centuries. As the Czech Republic is a relatively small country, many castles can be visited in one day, and many are in easy reach of the capital city of Prague. Tours are livened up by guides in historical costumes, accompanied by period music and dance, swordsmen, and falconers.

Arts and Architecture

Due in large part to Prague's place in history as a bridge between East and West, a wide variety of art and architecture is on display throughout the city. Historic cathedrals stand side by side with gleaming modern structures along the city skyline.

Across the countryside, the Czech Republic boasts more than two thousand preserved or restored castles and châteaux, more than any other country in the world. These historic structures are an important piece of cultural heritage, and the government has taken important steps to preserve these national treasures while ensuring that they are largely open to the public.

Music, Film, and Literature

The Czech Republic has produced many notable talents whose work has left a lasting mark on the world stage.

Czech writers have made lasting contributions to world literature. Perhaps the best known Czech author is Franz Kafka. Kafka's haunting works, including *Metamorphosis* and *The Trial*, have become classics of literature studied and

ABOVE: *The site of Hluboká Castle dates to the thirteenth century. However, it reached its current appearance during the nineteenth century, when Johann Adolf II von Schwarzenberg ordered the reconstruction of the castle in the romantic style of England's Windsor Castle.*

Church of the Sacred Heart, Prague

Josip Plečnik (1872–1957) is something of an odd man out among twentieth-century architects. A few years ago, not many people had heard of him; now, he is increasingly seen as a remarkable genius with an apparently inexhaustible fund of ideas, but little sympathy for his own time.

Church of the Sacred Heart (1928–32) in Žižkov, a district somewhat removed from the tourist-packed historical area of Prague. Elements of Plecnik's romantic nationalism, religious devotion, historicism, rationality, and not least of all his bravura gift for design are all displayed in this extraordinary church, which, if it had been built forty or fifty years later might be described as postmodernist.

It is most remarkable from the outside. The first, immediate shock is the slab-like tower, almost as wide as the basilica it adorns, and whose

restrained pediment it repeats. In the center of the tower, in a touch of surrealism, is a huge circular opening that contains a see-through clock. The lower part of the basilica and tower is brick, the upper parts, together with doorways, plastered white. The building is simple yet decorative, with Classical swags above the rows of small, almost-square windows, and vertical lines of projecting

interpreted in universities around the world. Milan Kundera, best known for his book *The Unbearable Lightness of Being*, is recognized as one of the best contemporary writers in the world. Playwright Václav Havel was elected president of Czechoslovakia in 1989 and in 1993 became the first president of the Czech Republic.

Czechs today enjoy music of all styles, including hip-hop, rock, and most other types of popular music. In addition, Czech culture has produced many great composers throughout history. The most widely recognized is the classical composer Antonín Dvořák.

ABOVE: *Franz Kafka.*

ABOVE: *Antonín Dvořák.*

ABOVE: *Milan Kundera.*

ABOVE: *Miloš Forman.*

Czechs have been successful in more modern artistic pursuits as well. Josef Sudek was known for his groundbreaking work in photography. Miloš Forman has received two Academy Awards for his work as a director. Forman received wide acclaim for his films *One Flew Over the Cuckoo's Nest* and *Amadeus*.

Festivals and Events

Holidays and festivals in the Czech Republic are celebrated with great enthusiasm. Traditional holidays reflect the diverse influences that have molded Czech culture through the centuries.

The Czech government honors eight national holidays. Some of these, like New Year's Day, Labor Day, Independence Day, and Christmas, are not

ABOVE: *In Prague, the carnival season is at the end of February and beginning of March. It is a colorful showcase of wonderful ideas, refined taste, and dazzling creativity.*

celebrated much differently in the Czech Republic than they are in other countries. Easter is a national holiday, but unlike the United States, the Czech Republic celebrates Easter Monday. On Easter Monday a special custom called *Pomlázka* is observed, where men swat their favorite women with decorated willow switches. This is supposed to bring new life to the land. Then little boys

ABOVE: *Burning of the Witches Night takes place every year on April 30. Its purpose is to celebrate the end of winter. Bonfires are lit and effigies of witches burned. This is said to drive out evil spirits.*

visit all the little girls they know and beg for gifts of candy and painted eggs. Later in the day, adult men go around to all the women in the village, but instead of candy, they receive shots of alcohol.

Other festivals are important to Czech culture but are not recognized as official government holidays. These include the Burning of the Witches, held each year in April, and the Festival Jiein, held in September. The Burning of the Witches is a pre-Christian festival where all-night bonfires are held to drive evil spirits out of the land. September's Festival Jičín, is a weeklong celebration that starts with a costumed parade. At the end of the parade, the mayor of the town holds a ceremony where he turns the town over to the children to run for the next week. Plays, concerts, parties, and educational exhibits are held throughout the festival, which ends with a fireworks display.

Text-Dependent Questions

1. Why are there so many atheists in the Czech Republic?

2. What is a *gymnázium?*

3. What is Pomlázka?

Research Project

Find out about Franz Kafka's life: where he was born, where he lived, and about his interest in Jewish religion and culture.

Words to Understand

textile: Woven or knitted cloth.

urban: Relating to a city.

water meadow: A field that is often flooded by water.

BELOW: The Church of Our Lady before Týn in Prague Old Town.

Chapter Five
THE FAMOUS CITIES OF THE CZECH REPUBLIC

The modern Czech Republic is an **urban** society with most of its citizens settling around the industry of its cities. Families are small, usually with only one or two children, and can be found living much as they are in most Western cities. Apartment complexes are a common and growing answer to the nation's housing needs, and modern apartment buildings can be found all over the Czech Republic.

Most Czech cities are small or medium sized; Prague, the capital, is the only truly large city. Throughout all Czech cities, one can find an interesting mix of old and new, giving Czech cities a unique character.

Prague

Prague is the Czech capital and the republic's largest city. It is also the acknowledged center of Czech history and culture. Cathedrals, bridges, and churches of varying ages and architectural styles can be found side by side throughout the city. The city hosts several international art and music festivals each year and has become one of the most visited cities in all of Europe.

ABOVE: *St. Vitus is a Roman Catholic metropolitan cathedral in Prague, the seat of the Archbishop of Prague.*

St. Nicholas, Prague

The church of St. Nicholas and the Jesuit College in Prague, in the Malá Strana or Lesser Town between the castle and the river, is the finest of all Bohemian baroque churches. The Jesuits decided to rebuild their Gothic church at the end of the seventeenth century and the first period of construction lasted from 1703 to 1711. The architect was Christoph Dientzenhofer (1655–1722), a member of the second generation of a famous Bavarian family settled in Prague. He completed the west facade and much of the nave before work was interrupted, no doubt by money problems. Work resumed in 1737 under Christoph's famous son, Kilian Ignaz, who was responsible for the mighty dome and drum, and the adjacent tower that dominates the Malá Strana, likened by the irreverent to a fat lady dancing with a thin man. The structure was largely completed by 1755, after Kilian Ignaz's death. The reason for building from west to east was to preserve the Gothic sanctuary until the last moment.

Even by the standards of the late baroque, this is one of the most dramatic of churches, largely the result of the striking color scheme of pink, green, and cream, and the flowing, rhythmic quality characteristic of the whole building. The walls almost disappear in the wealth of galleries, balconies, niches, and doorways. There is no insistent point of focus, but the eye is drawn to the

fabulous rococo pulpit constructed by the Prachners (a local workshop), the immense, almost threatening figures of Church Fathers, and the massive high altar with the figure of St. Nicholas, a popular church patron in Prague. By contrast, the dome over the choir is restrained and ethereal, while in the nave Johann Lukas Kracker's huge illusionist fresco of the life of St. Nicholas, painted in the 1760s, has been described as "one of the finest expressions of baroque monumental painting north of the Alps."

Educational Video

A sightseeing guide to the magical city of Prague.

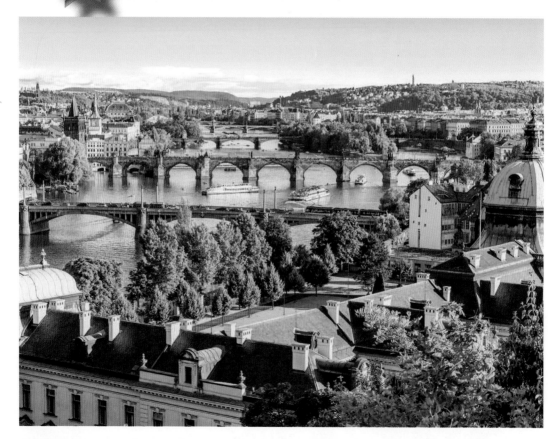

ABOVE: *A view of Prague Old Town. The second bridge from the front is the famous Charles Bridge.*

ABOVE: *Cathedral of St. Peter & Paul as seen from Špilberk Castle, Brno.*

Brno

The biggest Moravian city and the second-largest city in the Czech Republic, Brno lies in a wide valley, surrounded on three sides by mountains. Brno was founded on an important trade route, and its location has always been an advantage for its citizens: Brno is connected both with the industrial area to the north and with the agricultural and wine-growing areas toward the west and south. Home to several industries, including most of the Czech **textile** industries, Brno also offers beautiful surroundings and cultural sites of historical and artistic value.

Ostrava

Ostrava is the third-largest city in the Czech Republic. Located in northern Moravia, the first records of settlement date from the thirteenth century, when the so-called Amber Route, an important trade artery, led through the area from the Baltic Coast to the Mediterranean. The settlement started to develop quickly in the eighteenth century, when coal deposits were discovered, and rapid growth occurred in the twentieth century. Ostrava has become an important cultural, trade, and sporting center. The dominant feature of the city is the unique lower area of Vítkovice, which is included on the European Cultural Heritage List.

ABOVE: *Jirasek Square, Ostrava.*

ABOVE: *Poruba is an administrative district in the city of Ostrava. It lies in the Silesian part of the city. Much of its architecture dates from the 1950s. It was inspired by Soviet designs and town planning.*

ABOVE: *The Michal Mine, known by its Czech name Důl Michal in Ostrava-Michálkovice, is a museum of mining located in the pit bank of a former coal mine.*

Silesian Ostrava Castle

Silesian Ostrava Castle is situated in the north eastern industrial city of Ostrava. It dates back to the thirteenth century. The castle stands on a small hill at the confluence of the Lučina and Ostravice rivers. The castle was built for military purposes due to its proximity to the Polish border. In 1534, the Gothic castle was rebuilt into a renaissance château. It burned down in 1872 but was rebuilt. It was restored recently after many years of dilapidation, caused by the collapse of coal mining tunnels underground. Today, the castle is one of the most important tourist attractions in the city. The cellars have been converted into a freshwater fish aquarium. The castle also hosts various exhibitions and family events.

Coal mining within the city was stopped in 1994. Despite Ostrava's industrial history, it boasts a surprising amount of green space. Within the city boundaries lie the picturesque Polanka forest and meadows. The park includes lakes and water meadows.

Pilsen

Pilsen (Plzeň in Czech), a small Bohemian city of 170,000 people, is an important commercial, cultural, and industrial center. Primarily known for its famous breweries and the heavy machinery engineered and produced in the nearby Škoda Works, Pilsen is considered to be to an important educational center by Czechs. Besides its many elementary and secondary schools, it is the home to the University of West Bohemia and the Medical Faculty of Charles University. The most promient sites in Pilsen are the Gothic St. Bartholomew's Cathedral, the Renaissance town hall, and the Great Synagogue, which is the second-largest synagogue in Europe. A popular tourist destination is the Plzeňský Prazdroj Brewery, where visitors can take a tour to discover the history of beer making in the region. Pilsen was designated the European Capital of Culture in 2015, along with Mons in Belgium.

ABOVE: *Baroque architecture in the old town of Pilsen.*

ABOVE: *Not far from Pilsen is the baroque convent of Chotěšov.*

Text-Dependent Questions

1. How many children are there in most Czech families?

2. What is the capital city of the Czech Republic?

3. What products are famously produced in Pilsen?

Research Project

Prague has long been one of Central Europe's most historically rich cities. Write an essay about the history of Prague's architecture and culture through the centuries.

Words to Understand

lignite: A brownish-black type of coal.

pollution: Substances which make land, water, and air dirty or unsafe.

scholarship: Grants-in-aid to a student.

BELOW: Kohútka in the Zlín region, is a ski resort that is popular with tourists. It is situated on the border between Slovakia and the Czech Republic.

Chapter Six
A BRIGHT FUTURE
FOR THE CZECH REPUBLIC

Despite its long cultural history, the Czech Republic is a very new country. In fact, it is not even 30 years old!

Cultural Preservation

The Czechs have a lot to offer the future. Some of the world's best-known artists, writers, and musicians come from this region. The government has done its best to keep the arts afloat during various periods of economic difficulty endured over the decades.

The Czech Republic is supposed to use at least 1 percent of the state budget for cultural preservation, regardless of which political party is in power. Heritage

ABOVE: *EU and Czech Republic flags flying side by side.*

ABOVE: *The Czech Republic, despite being in the European Union, has kept its own currency (the koruna) like other countries such as Sweden and the UK.*

conservation, performing arts, and art education are mostly supported from public budgets, while the market-oriented branches such as the arts, press, media, architecture, and advertising are financed by companies and households. Government policy ensures that culture is officially recognized as a priority when producing its budget. The government also offers **scholarships** to students wishing to pursue the arts as a career. This new policy has not been around long enough to see the lasting effects. However, the fact that these policies are being created means that the government is taking the issue seriously. There is enthusiasm for the future.

The Environment

The Czech Republic suffers from air, water, and land **pollution** caused by industry, mining, and agriculture. Lung cancer is common in areas with the highest air pollution levels. In the mid-1990s, the nation had the world's highest

Czech Republic's Economy

Under communism, the old Czechoslovakia had been one of the most highly industrialized areas of Eastern Europe. Private ownership of the land in Czech Republic has gradually increased, and crops including hops, grains, and fruits are grown. There are reserves of coal, uranium, iron ore, and other minerals, and machinery and vehicles are produced for export. The Czech Republic is a member of the EU and greatly benefits from being part of it. However, it is notable that the country uses its own currency, the Czech koruna, and has not joined the euro. Economically, the Czech Republic is a success story. It has very low unemployment, a very low poverty rate, and a budget surplus.

ABOVE: *Chodov Business Park in Prague, which is completely made of steel and glass.*

carbon dioxide emissions, totaling 135.6 million metric tons per year. The country also had its air contaminated by sulphur dioxide emissions from the use of **lignite** as an energy source in the former Czechoslovakia. Other Western nations have offered the Czech Republic $1 billion to spur environmental reforms, but the pressure to continue economic growth has postponed the government's push for environmental action. Poor air quality is a major problem in the country. Acid rain has destroyed much of the forest in the northern part of the country. Farming and mining have caused land erosion. Recent efforts include the closing of several lignite mines and stricter enforcement of environmental regulations. Environmental considerations have also led government officials to consider nuclear energy as a main source of power for the country's future.

ABOVE: *Tourists and locals alike enjoying a fall market at Wenceslas Square in Prague.*

ABOVE: Jezeří Castle in the north of Bohemia has the unusual backdrop of a lignite mine. The burning of this unrefined resource has caused pollution on a large scale.

Catching Up

As of today, the Czech Republic has not set a date to join the euro, however, it is generally considered that it will not be adopted until at least 2020. Officials have stated that fixing the country's economic structure is currently a bigger priority. Adopting the euro could help improve the economy through increased trade with other member countries of the Eurozone, although the future of the euro itself is somewhat in doubt as the EU shoulders through recent recessions.

The EU is also committed to environmental protection, and once again, the Czech Republic lags behind. The EU aims to have 20 percent of all energy produced by member states come from renewable energy sources. The Czech Republic is far behind this goal. Almost 60 percent of energy within the nation comes from coal, which takes a heavy toll on the environment. Another 30 percent comes from nuclear plants, which also present dangers to the environment. The Czech Republic hopes to have at least 13 percent of all energy come form renewable sources by 2020.

The Czech Republic now generates clean energy in many forms including: hydro, biomass, solar, and wind, thereby making a major contribution toward meeting its obligations toward the European Union. In the future, the country plans to build more renewable facilities throughout the country.

The Czech Republic has a long way to go to catch up with the rest of the EU, but it has come a long way in a short time. There's hope for its future!

ABOVE: *The Czech Republic is taking steps to improve air quality by installing photovoltaic power stations, such as this one near Pilsen.*

ABOVE: *A biomass plant at a pig farm in the Czech Republic.*

Text-Dependent Questions

1. What does the Czech government do to protect Czech culture and arts?

2. What illness can be caused by pollution?

3. When will the Czech Republic adopt the euro?

Research Project

How many sources of renewable energy does the Czech Republic use? Describe how each kind of renewable energy is generated.

400 BCE	Celts occupy Czech lands.
600 CE	Slavic peoples fully inhabit the region.
900	The Přemyslid dynasty family begins to establish the Bohemian Kingdom.
1355	Prague becomes the new imperial city for the Holy Roman Empire.
1526	The Habsburg Dynasty takes control of the Bohemian throne.
1914	World War I begins.
1918	Czechoslovakia proclaims itself an independent democratic state.
1938	Czechoslovakia surrenders the Sudetenland to Germany.
1939	Hitler invades the remainder of Czechoslovakia.
1945	Czechoslovakia is liberated from Nazi occupation and reestablishes democratic rule.
1948	Soviets cement Communist control of Czechoslovakia.
1968	The Prague Spring reform movement is put down by Soviet troops.
1989	The Velvet Revolution takes hold and Communist rule ends.
1990	First free elections held since 1942.
1993	The Czech Republic separates from the former Czechoslovakia.
2003	Czechs pass a referendum supporting membership in the EU.
2004	The Czech Republic is admitted to the EU.
2006	President Klaus appoints a center-right government led by Mirek Topolánek of the Civic Democratic Party (ODS in Czech).
2007	The Czech Republic joins the EU's Schengen Treaty free movement zone.
2010	ODS leader Petr Nečas forms a coalition government with the right-wing TOP 09 party and the centrist Public Affairs party.
2013	New government headed by Jiří Rusnok loses a confidence vote in parliament. MPs vote to dissolve parliament, paving the way for early elections.
2016	"Czechia" is officially confirmed as an alternative short English name for the Czech Republic.

Further Reading

Baker, Mark. Wilson, Neil. *Lonely Planet Prague & the Czech Republic* (Travel Guide). London: Lonely Planet Publications, 2017.

David, Petr. Dobrovodsky, Vladimir. Lowry, Nicholas. Phillimore, Polly. Turner-Kadeckova, Joy. Turp, Craig. *DK Eyewitness Travel Guide: Prague.* London: DK, 2017.

McCormick, John. *Understanding the European Union: A Concise Introduction.* London: Palgrave Macmillan, 2017.

Mason, David S. *A Concise History of Modern Europe: Liberty, Equality, Solidarity.* London: Rowman & Littlefield, 2015.

Internet Resources

Czech Republic Country Profile
http://www.bbc.co.uk/news/world-europe-17220018

Czech Tourism
https://www.czechtourism.com/home/

Lonely Planet: Czech Republic
https://www.lonelyplanet.com/czech-republic

The Official Website of the European Union
europa.eu/index_en.htm

Publisher's note:
The websites listed on this page were active at the time of publication. The publisher is not responsible for websites that have changed their addresses or discontinued operation since the date of publication. The publisher will review and update the website list upon each reprint.

INDEX

Video Credits

Page 12 Geography Now!: http://x-qr.net/1Heq
page 24 Victoria's Channel: http://x-qr.net/1HBd
page 46 CzechInvest: http://x-qr.net/1GL9
page 55 HONEST GUIDE: http://x-qr.net/1Eyr
page 72 Expedia: http://x-qr.net/1EuP

Author

Dominic J. Ainsley is a freelance writer on history, geography, and the arts and the author of many books on travel. His passion for traveling dates from when he visited Europe at the age of ten with his parents. Today, Dominic travels the world for work and pleasure, documenting his experiences and encounters as he goes. He lives in the south of England in the United Kingdom with his wife and two children.